D1415079

To Sebastian

This book officially signed by the author:

Love,

Grandpa Janka

_____
Ed Janka

I hope that you enjoy reading my stories as
much as I have enjoyed living them!

I Never Had
a
Bike:

Tales of Basketball and Life

by
ED JANKA

WITH BOB BROWN

FOREWORD BY COACH BOB KNIGHT

I Never Had a Bike:
Tales of Basketball and Life
by Ed Janka

Published by:

Brown Book Company (BBC) Limited
65 Crockford Blvd.
Toronto, ON
M1R 3B7
www.brownbook.ca

Print ISBN: 978-0-9692805-1-4
eBook ISBN: 978-0-9692805-2-1

*For my beautiful wife Louise.
So that she doesn't have to listen to these
stories anymore!*

Table of Contents

Foreword

Ed Janka has for many years been an innovator and a great contributor to the game of basketball.

Through his nationwide clinics on the game he has brought the best coaches to discuss and teach the various aspects of the game. There is nothing that his clinics do not cover about the game of basketball.

The coaches that make up his clinics discuss, demonstrate and provide a great look at the intricacies of the game. His clinics always attract the best coaches and teachers the game has to offer such as Tara Vanderveer and Geno Auriemma.

There is no single person that has done more for the development of the game of basketball than Ed Janka.

I have greatly enjoyed working with Ed over these many years.

Bob Knight

Introduction

Before you ask me about the title, it was just something that came up one day in a conversation and it ended up as the title of the book.

As a kid I grew up in Chicago and I had plenty of things to do, but riding a bike wasn't one of them. It was a good thing, too. Because, as the title says, I never had a bike.

You may be wondering why I wrote this book.

All of these stories I have told many times before. My lovely wife Louise has heard them so many times she often excuses herself and leaves the room when I start talking (not to mention rolling her eyes or screaming once in a while)!

Well, I have a friend, Bob Brown who I originally met at the Vince Carter Fantasy Camp in Toronto back in 2002. Coincidentally, Bob and I ended up living in the same condo building in Florida (maybe he's a stalker). Bob kept telling me that I should write some of the stories down, that they would make a great book.

Well, finally we decided to do just that. He and I, over the course of a few months, sat together while he recorded the stories as I told them all one more time.

Coincidentally, Bob is in the printing business. He kept telling me that he only prints books, he doesn't write them. But eventually, after recording the stories, he put them into a book format and he printed a few copies for me.

Bob said that if I sold some, I could buy him a drink or two at the Tiki bar on the beach near our condo building. We'll see about that.

Anyway, I hope you enjoy the stories and if you come across any mistakes, errors, typos or blatant lies…well, just blame Bob, he obviously didn't hear me properly or we had too many Crown Royals that day.

Jimmy V and Dr Love

The great coach Jim Valvano and I got to be very close friends. He knew that I really loved music! One day he called me up when I was at Nike and said we are hosting the Beach Music Awards Festival. It's a shag thing, it's a south east coast thing, they love to shag, which is a swing style dance. He asked me down, and he says we're going to be co-presenters. What am I doing? Co-presenters? He said I want you to be there with me.

Because there were so many acts, they couldn't get them all into the Reynolds Coliseum. So they had these large RVs which every group or performer was going to be in. We are sitting there in our own RV and Jimmy asks "you know who's in the RV next to us?" I said "who?" Jimmy says "the Prince of Pillow talk, Dr. Love himself...Barry White!" The guy was huge at this time and I don't just mean physically. He makes everyone feel good with his music style.

We're sitting there having a drink, I asked Jimmy if we can go over there and meet him? Jimmy said why not? Jimmy was always a 'Why not guy', he felt at that time in his life he could get in to see anybody. Presidents, whoever...he had walls of pictures and mementos in his office.

So we go over and knocked on his door. I hear this very deep voice say "Hello?" Jimmy says it's Jimmy Valvano. "Jim!" Barry responds, "come on in".

We go in and we are sitting with the master! He's in a big robe. I mean a big robe, he's big. But, he was such a nice guy. A friend of mine from Cleveland loved Barry so I had a program signed for him. We talked for a while with him about all kinds of things. I found out that most of the greats, whatever they are into, whether it be a sport, or music are always really nice people. Especially when they don't have their 400 "hangers-on" with them.

All of a sudden there was another knock at the door and a voice said "Mr. White, you're on in five". Well let me tell you, for a big man he sure could move. He was out of his chair and ready to change into his outfit in no time. He then excused himself and proceeded to get ready for his show.

A great guy and a true gentleman!

The Italian Job

Early in my career I replaced an Italian coach in Cagliari on the Island of Sardinia. Which wasn't easy, but I had black hair at the time, so maybe I had the Italian look. A lot of good stories with good people happened and when the season was over they paid me, in my world at that time, very well. They owed me about 16,000 American dollars.

We had just lost our playoff game and Dr. Carlo Pirastu, who was in charge, threw a big season-ending party that night. I was supposed to leave the next day. During the party Dr. Pirastu called me into his office to pay me.

He proceeds to give me the $16,000 in tens, fives and ones! At the time it was a difficult thing to take that home because you can only take $3,000 out of the country. So I take it and I thought "oh my God what am I going to do?" The party ended with the owner at around midnight and I had a 6am flight.

I started to think about how I am going to get this money back? I need to have the money because I was a single guy at that time and I had responsibilities and bills to pay.

There was a movie out around that time called Midnight Express where this kid got caught with dope going in to some country. I started to figure out that I need to tape that money to me, just like the drug smuggler did in the movie. I took all the bigger bills and taped them to my body. Remember these were different times, you could not get away with this in today's airports.

So I have the money, the trophy that they gave me and my luggage, I got on the plane to Rome. When we landed I have to go through customs and security before flying back to the U.S. In front of me there's an innocent looking American couple with two young children and they take them aside and search them like they were a problem.

I'm sweating now, worried that they're about to find out what I'm doing. It's time for me to go through and all of a sudden they start yelling "*grande allenatore Janka*" which means "great coach Janka". They recognized me from the games and waved me through.

I nervously smiled, breathed a sigh of relief, went through and high tailed to the bathroom and took all the sweat stained money I had off my body and put it in my case.

What a relief!

Love and Basketball

There's a story that I heard that the outstanding Coach and friend Rick Majerus was traveling with Coach Al McGuire in the car on a long road trip and they're talking about basketball and life and everything else. Rick turns to Al and said that he was dating a new girl and he was having a little trouble in his relationship with the girl.

Al asks Rick, well what is it, is it a communication thing, are you keeping things from her? Rick said no.

Al asks, well is it a bedroom problem, a problem with the sexual situation, he said no, that's fine.

Well what is it, Al finally says? Rick pauses and slowly says: she just doesn't love the game.

And that's who Rick was, he loved the game and the game was more important in his life than anything since the time he was 12 years old.

That's true love!

The Right Place at the Right Time

George Koehler, a wonderful guy and one of Michael Jordan's best friends, told me this story at one of Michael's camps. In 1984, when Chicago had drafted Michael as the third overall pick, he flew into Chicago from Raleigh Durham. Believe it or not, the Bulls had neglected to send anyone out to the airport to pick up Michael.

George Koehler had his own limo service at the time. Michael flies in, George is looking for some other person and waiting and waiting. His guy does not come in that he's waiting for.

George is a basketball guy and there's Michael coming off the plane and there's no one from the Bulls waiting for him.

As a big fan and a former high school ball player himself, George recognized Michael immediately. George offered him a ride and they bonded right away. He showed him around the city and took him to his hotel.

It developed into a great friendship that has lasted to this day. He is a tough, good guy that Michael trusts. He would've taken a cab if George wasn't there, but fate thought otherwise.

He just happened to be in the right place at the right time.

It's on me!

We were in Kansas City for a clinic and there's Coach Jerry Tarkanian, Coach Jim Valvano, just a great list of coaches. We were eating at an Italian restaurant, usually I got the check, because I was with Nike and these were our coaches.

We're having a great time, it's good, everyone's telling stories, it's a real nice evening. Near the end of the evening P.J. Carlesimo says "I've got the check". I was a little surprised, but said great, thanks a lot. All the guys thank him and we all head out.

So the next week after the clinic was over, all of the coaches, I think there were about twelve, send in their expense reports for travel and so on. P.J. has a short list and I am looking it over and it has the dinner on it!

So I called him and said P.J. what are you doing? He responds: "I got the check, you got the check. It's all good!" He looks like the hero, I take the fall!

Got me!

Did you hear the one about…

Back in the late eighties I thought that we needed entertainment for the coaches trip that we take every year. Carol Vaughn was the person that ran all the Nike trips for the different coaches of different sports. I told her that and she said, "Well I'm going to give you some video tapes of some different comedians for you to look at."

I was talking with Jimmy Valvano on the phone and told him that they were looking at a certain hot comedian by the name of Jerry Seinfeld, he said, "This guy is the greatest, he was the best guy that you could ever have." I said, "OK I'm with you." Then I saw him on the Johnny Carson Show, he was really young but he was very talented. I'm getting pushed to make a decision so I called and said, "Carol, let's get Seinfeld."

So we are in Carmel, California in the late 80s before Jerry was the giant that he is today. Carol calls and says that he is coming in, he wants to sit down with a few of the coaches and you and have dinner. We have the dinner and it's really nice, there's Tony Barone, who's my best friend, his wife Kathy, Jimmy and his wife Pam and a couple of the other coaches and their wives.

Jerry sits at the end of the table, there's only like 8 or 10 people. You expect a guy that's a comedian to be funny, but he barely said two words. Jimmy being Jimmy, took over the whole thing, all of sudden it's the Jim Valvano table and he had us all laughing!

We go through the evening and Jimmy and I meet for a drink later and he says, "God, that guy, I thought he would be great. But I'm not sure now"

I said "Jimmy I'm really concerned about this thing tomorrow night" I said, "You're the one who told me to get him!" Jimmy said "don't worry, he will knock it out tomorrow night"

The next night is the big wrap up night. We have a jazz band that plays for the group, 120 coaches and their wives. I have to go up to give a little introduction which

Carol Vaughn gave me. So I introduce him, and Jerry comes out.

I'm at a table with Jimmy and his wife. We are sitting there and believe me, this guy is bombing; he's not very funny. I lean over to Jim and say, "Jim, this guy is terrible." He says, "well, we have to do something!" He then says, "meet me in the lobby." He said, "I'm going to walk out, 30 seconds later you walk out."

So we leave, I say, "Jim this guy's horrible. I mean no one is laughing at this thing." He says, "here's what we're going to do, we are going to stand in the dark at the back of the ballroom and when Jerry says anything, we're going to laugh, long and loud. We will get other people laughing." I said, "Do you really want to do this?" "Yep!" he replied.

So we go back there and that's what we do, and we laugh and laugh and laugh. People start looking around wondering what is happening. Then the whole room started to laugh along with us. Jimmy has a distinct laugh and people were either laughing at Jimmy's laugh or laughing because we were.

And it was all about not letting this, at the time, young comedian bomb. Finally we went back to our own seats. I said to Jimmy, this guys not going to make it big.

Little did I know. He went on to be one of the greatest comedians of all time!

Polish Luck

During one of the Michael Jordan Senior Flight School Fantasy Camps, we were in Vegas and my wife Louise and I went to go see the Temptations. This is a while ago and when we get out it's close to midnight. We come back and the campers always had a special place reserved in the casino at that time to gamble.

Well, Michael's at a table, he's by himself playing two hands and he's obviously not doing well. I sat down and just wanted to say hello and goodnight before heading for my room after a long day. He tells me the cards haven't been in his favor that evening and he is down a lot.

I said I will have a drink but I'm not playing. All of a sudden he starts winning, it's getting good everything is great, he's making money and that's good. I'm happy for him but I'm tired and I've got to get up early and run the camp.

So he's rolling and things are going really well. So I get up to leave and Michael says "what are you doing?"

I said I'm going. I have to go. He said no, not now, you have to stay with me. His winning streak just kept going as I sat there watching and just being his Polish lucky charm. Eventually, I managed to slip away and head up to my room.

He came into the camp right on time the next morning, but I could tell he had been up all night. I asked how he did and he gave me a big smile and a 'thumbs up'!

I guess I really was his lucky charm, that time at least!

One of a Kind

Let me talk to you a little about Al McGuire. I could talk all day about what a great coach he was, but before we get to the coaching things let's talk about what he's like as a man.

He taught more guys about being a man then they ever thought they could be. Marquette University would never have had the success that they had through the years if it wasn't for Al McGuire. I think that Al was a person that was way ahead of his time. I was fortunate enough to know him and, God bless his soul, carry his casket.

He was a real motivator and touched the lives and affected every person that played for him, worked with him or even came in touch with him over the years.

Al was one of college basketball's most successful coaches for 20 years, leading Marquette to 11 postseason appearances, winning an NCAA title in 1977.

I think that people should try and understand what he was all about. He was about making people better and making the university better.

I think we should try to understand that the life of Al McGuire is the life of Marquette basketball.

I've known a lot of great people over the years, but Al was one of a kind!

Just Do It

When I was at Marquette, I really wanted to coach. I just thought it was a good time to do something I really wanted to do. I wasn't a great player, but I was just the kind of guy that wanted to coach. An opportunity came along and I became a grad assistant at Marquette and then got a job at John Carroll University thanks to Al McGuire.

I love to coach and I had a passion for it. So I went from coaching at John Carroll to coaching in Italy. Then I coached two years at the University of Detroit as an assistant, one year at Oberlin College and four years assisting at Fairfield University. Then it was time for the biggest change in my life.

I didn't have a job and all of a sudden I have two opportunities. I had been offered a coaching position at

Creighton University with my best friend Tony Barone and the folks at Nike had approached me about joining them.

I could've been an assistant coach but I was so tired of the coaching game. It was time for a new direction. I just was not happy with what's going on in coaching. I felt that my job should not depend on someone else. So I went to Nike and it became the best thing that ever happened for sure.

As the great folks at Nike say, Just Do It..and I did!

Ahead of His Time

A lot of people might not want to hear this, they might think that I'm dissing my father and I would never do that. But Al McGuire was the most important man in my life! Through my late teens, right through to before he passed, which was when I was into my mid 50s. I consider him as close as I could be to a second father. He did so much more for me than I ever did for him. I think he saw something in me, and I am who I am and most of it's because of him.

He kind of set the tone for me, and it wasn't about the coaching or basketball. It's more about what he wanted to see, he saw potential in people and he could see what they were capable of. Regardless of whether that was a player, a manager or a friend.

He was just so ahead of his time. I don't think there's anybody who knew more about the business of basketball than Al McGuire. The millions of dollars that coaches make today, in the NBA or college, I'm not saying he made that happen, but he set a tone that you shouldn't be ashamed to make money while you're working hard and coaching the game.

Al felt that if the university is making money, the coach should share in it. In the fall, college football stadiums are full with 50, 60, 70 thousand and more. In the winter college basketball arenas have 10, 15, 20 thousand in attendance and don't forget the TV money.

They're selling out arenas for the NCAA tournament, it's the greatest sporting event spread out over a four week period, not just one day. He saw all of that stuff way ahead of his time. He taught people how to use their talents to go beyond who they were.

I believed in him and his philosophy. I was not a great or even a good basketball player, I just liked to hang on and create friendships through basketball. He was someone that would teach you and encouraged you as well. He convinced me that I had some type of talent that I could use.

Let's Go Camping

I had just joined Nike and met Michael Jordan which was the start of something special for me. A little while later there was a dinner of eight or ten people to celebrate Michael's success personally and in his partnership with Nike.

Sonny Vacarro, who was in charge of basketball at Nike and was involved in signing Michael to his first deal there, was part of the group. Sonny mentions to Michael that he should have his own basketball camp. Suggesting to Michael that I should direct his camp—what a life changing moment!

Michael and I got together and set up a kids' camp. We did the first camp in Wilmington, North Carolina and then moved the camp to Chicago, where we held it for fourteen more years.

Meanwhile, I saw that there was a Laker adult fantasy camp in Hawaii, I'm not sure who set that up. I asked Michael, he was probably around 24 years old, what do you think about an adult fantasy camp? Michael right away said, well I'm too young.

Not many guys would say that that they're too young. But Michael knew that he wasn't ready. He was smart enough to realize that the time was not right for him to do that type of camp.

Two years later he came to me and said he was ready and let's do it. So we discussed the details and he said he wanted it to be at a great venue, a place that people wanted to go to, he wanted it to be fun and he wanted to have the greatest coaches that are available.

We did get the best coaches including many hall of famers and future hall of famers. The funny thing was, I think that they enjoyed it as much as the players did. Year after year, it was just a fun event for everyone involved.

George Raveling, a former college coach and a Nike executive, joined me at the camp. As it developed it became just one of the greatest experiences of my life. I got to know Michael really well. I found out that he is not just the greatest basketball player ever, but a great human being, too!

The camp attracted a wide range of participants. Some real big-money guys attended. Everyone wanted to play with Michael. We even had NBA owner, Mark Cuban there for two years. It was just a wonderful time!

I didn't have many complaints from the 'campers'. Michael always made it special for all of the 'campers'. He would talk to them about basketball, of course. But he would also talk about their jobs, finance, travel and whatever else they were interested in. Because Michael was interested in learning from them, too, it turns out.

Definitely one of the greatest experiences of my life!

The Czar

Mike Fratello is one of the most interesting and quality coaches that I've ever met. He and I met through Chuck Dailey and Rollie Massimino. Mike is a great coach of the style that will always keep his teams in the game, always giving them a chance to win.

He's also a great speaker, motivator and a TV analyst. Mike is a single guy and enjoys life a lot with the many friends in both the collegiate world and I'd say even more so in the NBA.

He is just one of those guys that has always been a good friend to me. Whenever I've asked him to speak he always comes through.

Quick little story about him, he did speak for me in Cleveland, he came off the road from somewhere to speak on a panel. He shows up and the first thing he says is that he needs to iron his clothes for the presentation. He ironed his Polo shirt and even his warm-ups! He was always impeccably dressed and always looked great! Mike is someone that I admire because he could stand the test of time.

He always sends me something for Christmas, and each time it's different and unique…and most of all it's always a fun thing. One year he sent me bottles of root beer with "Janka's Root Beer" labels on it.

He's one of those guys who is thoughtful, and knows many, many people. It's a long list in regards to who he knows, and for me to be part of that list is pretty nice.

It's hard to not like Mike.

Getting His Point Across

Coach McGuire made things happen that no one ever dreamt of. In 1970 I think there were only 32 teams in the NCAA. They wanted to send us to Fort Worth, Texas to play. Al said how are our fans going to get there? We can't get close to Fort Worth Texas? So he refused to go. You think that would ever happen today? He was ahead of his time. He was the guy that a lot of coaches and a lot of people admired.

When we went to the NCAA tournament in Minneapolis, Minnesota it was the only stadium that has a raised court. You sat below the court. The locker rooms are even more below the court. We were about to play Kentucky when Adolph Rupp was the coach. I'm on the staff, a grad assistant. We're in the locker room, Kentucky being all white players, Al is using that kind of thing to our advantage.

Al's starts his pregame talk saying "he wouldn't recruit you" to the different players. And the players you can see are getting really hostile especially the New York guys. He gets them all sitting down, getting ready and assistant Hank Raymond has got all the stuff on the board.

All of a sudden there's a knock at the door of the locker room. This kid comes in, a little kid, 5 foot 10, glasses, he's wearing a Kentucky sweater, it has manager at the bottom. He says "Coach McGuire, Coach Rupp would like to know which basket you're going to shoot at." Al said "tell Rupp, we'll shoot wherever we want to and to go F@#* himself." This young kid, well his eyes went wide open, he was in a stance, says OK and runs out the door! I know the players are like wow and the black players are like holy shit.

We ended up losing the game by a point. Quite a game. Our guys fought hard throughout. Coach and everyone out there put their best game forward.

If you look at years earlier, Kentucky lost to Texas El Paso, who won a national championship with 5 black guys over Kentucky. What a story that was!

From Internet: Supposedly, the term "The Big Dance" was coined in 1977 by Marquette University's head coach, Al McGuire. McGuire wore a blue blazer the entire season and when asked by a reporter if he would continue wearing it in the NCAA tournament, he replied, "Absolutely. You gotta wear the blue blazer to the big dance." And his team went on to win the national championship that year. Thus, the phenomenon was born and we have run with it.

Thinking Out of the Box

Jimmy Valvano was as talented a person that ever coached. I don't mean a talented coach, and I don't mean a talented person. He was the most talented human being that was ever in the coaching profession. He had passion about what he did as a coach. He also had passion about what he could accomplish away from the game. Al McGuire used to always say that he admired Jimmy a great deal. He thought he was the second coming of him. He had a way about himself and he could do a lot more than just coach. He could win and do a lot of other things just as well.

Jimmy was a guy that you get attracted to. I don't care what life you're in, when he talked with you you wanted to listen and you wanted to talk to him. He was smart, he could do things that other people wouldn't dare to do. He would take chances. It was similar to when I worked at Nike, Phil Knight and the company were always playing on the edge. Jimmy was always on the edge, taking the chance to do something different.

When he coached he would put a 5 foot ten guard fronting a 7 foot center! Nine times out of ten his little guy would win!. He would do that, he would do something no coach would ever think about doing. Jimmy always wanted to try to do something different and off the charts.

I think that it was that out of the box thinking that made him so outstanding!

A Celebration of a Great Man

I was honored to be a pallbearer at Al McGuire's funeral. That cold day in Milwaukee, January 29th, 2001, was one of the most memorable and toughest experiences of my life.

Because we all gathered, the Marquette people, it was like a homecoming that none of us ever wanted to have. We went there on a typical Milwaukee winter day. Hard rain and snow, a terrible day and yet at the church, as Al would always talk about, all he wanted to do was sell it out, and he did!

He filled it out, there was no room, there was nothing, there were so many people and they were there because of him.

My only regret is I didn't see many college coaches there. That kind of personally upset me. They couldn't make time? They had games and I understand that but, come on, this was Al!

Hubie Brown shows up, he's doing games but he made time. Ray Meyer was there and there were many other people there that admired, and loved Al. I think to me it just shows what it was all about. It was a great moment. There was a huge reception at a golf course after. Friends and family retelling stories about Coach. Two days of celebrating his life because he was so remarkable.

Holding Their Attention

I had many coaches that spoke for me at our Nike Championship Basketball Clinics. My two "go-to" guys were Jimmy Valvano and Abe Lemons. When I set up the clinics, when they were both there or whether one was there, they were never going to speak any other time other than Friday night or Saturday night and always be the final speakers. They closed it out each evening, making those coaches who attended feel good about what they heard and experienced.

We had a clinic in Cleveland, Ohio back when I started my clinics in 1974. We're at the Sheraton Hopkins Airport Hotel. The room held maybe 500 to 550 people. Those were the days of coaches using overhead projectors. Not like today with people on the court. Abe spoke on Friday, and he was dynamite. Saturday Jimmy is supposed to speak at 8:15pm for an hour and 15 minutes. All of my clinic sessions are usually an hour and 15 minutes. I don't know why I think of that number but it seemed comfortable for all the guys that spoke. An hour is too short an hour and a half is too long.

It's Saturday around 5 o'clock and we break for dinner. I get a call up in the room and it's Jimmy. He says, "Ed I've got bad news, I've been delayed", he says "I'll get there, but I won't get there until about 10 o'clock".

So I said OK. You just get here as quick as you can, I'll take care of things. So I think what am I going to do? I can't get a substitute, there's no way. Jimmy was supposed to start around 8:15. The first speaker went on around 6:45, talking until 8 o'clock. So I'm talking to my people, so I say this is what we're going to do. We always had a hospitality hour on Friday and Saturday nights after the final speaker. Soda, beer, just guys enjoying themselves. So I said, OK I'm going to announce that after our first speaker we will have our hospitality hour from 8:00pm to 9:45pm and Jimmy will speak at 10:00pm.

Jimmy was a guy who drew people. It wasn't gonna be a problem. So we have the hospitality hour and everybody is loud and having a few drinks. Now they're back in the hall around 9:30. And they are everywhere. They're laying on the floor, the steps, they've had their beers but they're not rowdy, but it's just jammed packed.

Now it's close to 10 and I don't see Jimmy. I'm down there and I'm trying to hold off, I trust him with my life. Suddenly, he busts through the door, he's got his NC State warm-ups on. He's got a shoulder suit bag and a duffel bag. He runs into the room, he throws the stuff on the stage and he says: Ed give me that thing! As he pointed at the microphone.

Just like that, he starts talking. He went on for an hour and a half, mostly laughs and great stories, as he had these 500 or more people captive.

I'm sitting by the door and I'm watching and thinking these are people that just had some beers and some drinks and were whooping it up a short time ago. But he had their full attention. They're listening to this guy and they're laughing and having a good time. And I said that's what he's all about. He controlled the audience.

He was special.

Preparation!

Hubie Brown may be the greatest coach who has never won an NBA championship. Mind you, he's won an ABA championship.

There is no one who's ever been part of coaching the game, at any level that is not more prepared, and having come prepared and having his players prepared, mentally and physically more than than Hubie Brown.

What he does on TV for so many years, I think there are people who learn more about the game from Hubie Brown, the NBA game, then in books or videos that you watch. If you listen to him he'll tell you why this is happening and a lot of it is statistics. Which, if you think about it statistics make up a lot. It doesn't make it a truism for every moment. But it makes up a lot for what is happening on the court. And Hubie is a teacher he always talked about that, Just like Jack Ramsay, Bob Knight and Mike Krzyzewski. These guys have been teachers of the game. They don't want to go out and just have players play, they want to keep teaching players how to be better.

I'll never forget at the Jordan Fantasy Camp that Hubie started with us from the get-go. Michael loved Hubie Brown because he was a great teacher. Just like Dean Smith, another great teacher said, if you don't teach and just roll the ball out, you lose!

Hubie is just so intricate of a guy. When we did the Nike trips, there would be 100 or more great male and female coaches. Hubie would have a little coaches clinic. For a couple of hours a day, usually between other sessions. People knew it and they would come. We would have a small group of outstanding collegiate coaches there, and he would just do his thing. To have him speak to 25 to 35 coaches, when usually he speaks to 600 or 700 coaches, that is   special. He is a remarkable individual when it comes to coaching the game.

Wrong Call

Lenny Wilkins, was a guest speaker for me when I did a Fantasy Camp in Toronto.

He told a short story about his first year as a player in the league and a referee called a foul on him. Lenny turned to the referee and said: "I bet you wouldn't call that on me if I was an all-star".

And the ref said "son, you'll never have to worry about that".

He went on to be a great all-star player and a Hall of Fame player and coach. Winning more games than anyone else.

I guess the referee got that call wrong!

A Really Good Guy…Really!

I feel that Bob Knight has gotten much more amiable in the last 10 years. I would say the one thing I've learned about Bob in last six or seven years is that he loves to teach the game, more than ever!

I will tell you a well kept secret about Bob Knight, he has a really big heart!

One of the times Bob spoke he told me that he wanted me to give his fee to the library in Orrville, Ohio, where he was born and raised. They needed the money to keep the library going. I don't know how many people think about that when they're successful. To go back and think "sixty years ago, I was a high school kid there, they need help and I'm gonna do that".

I just think there's so much more to Bob Knight than the chair throw and other bullshit that happened. He is such a better person than that. I feel that if you asked another great coach, Mike Krzyzewski, he would say the same thing.

One of the great moments that I remember on TV was when Coach K got inducted into the Hall of Fame and Bob Knight was right there. Bob introduced him and they hugged. They've had their differences, but when it comes to showtime and things that are important and people lives, Bob Knight is there for his friends. I think he's just an outstanding guy.

Two years ago we had our 40th anniversary of doing clinics. Bob was at the clinic and he was kind enough to say some really great things about what I've done, and what I have tried to do to help basketball.

He didn't have to do that, but I think that he knows what should happen in the coaching profession and he's trying to make it better all the time. I think that Bob is a wonderful guy!

With Hall of Famer Dean Smith

With Purdue's greatest coach, Gene Keady

Talk about two winners!
Bob Knight and Geno Auriemma

Bob Huggins, Hubie Brown, Charlie Spoonhour,
Eric Lautenbach and Gene Keady

The Admiral David Robinson and (Sir) Charles Barkley

Bill Raftery, Billy Packer and Al McGuire

My friends, The Temptations

M.J. & my wife Louise

In Vegas Eric Lautenbach, P.J. Carlesimo, Coach K
and Marty Fletcher

With the great Hubie Brown

The Jankas and Coach Gary Williams

Hall of Famer John Chaney

Hall of Famer Jim Calhoun

Celtic great and Hall of Famer Sam Jones

Jimmy "V" before Beach Music Awards Presentations

Coach K (Just two kids from Chicago)

My best friend, Tony Barone

Alongside the greatest player of all time

P.J. Carlesimo

Al McGuire and some of Marquette's great players
Ric Cobb, Maurice Lucas, Jack Burke, Bo Ellis

Tennis Anyone?

I was at a grad assistant at Marquette in 1972/73. The head coaching job at John Carroll University, a Division III school, right outside of Cleveland, Ohio became open. I was very interested in the job, and Al McGuire made a call to the director about giving me an interview. I went up and interviewed and got the job.

The Athletic Director called me that evening and said can you come over tomorrow morning so we can go over your responsibilities. He said you came in for the basketball job but there's another thing that you're going to have to do, like teaching and coaching other sports. I said sure.

I was so excited to get the job, I was 26 at the time, I went into his office. He said, well you're obviously the coach, you're also in charge of the budget, you'll be teaching three activity classes, handball, racquetball and horseback riding.

I told him right away I've never been on a horse in my life. He said don't worry about it. It won't be your responsibility. What will happen is, at about 15 minutes before class starts the students will come to your office, and you will take attendance, and then you will walk all of them to the bus and they'll go to a riding stable and that's all you have to do.

Then he said that the other coaching job you have in the spring is coaching tennis. I told him that I've only banged around a tennis ball a little bit with my friends in college but I've never actually played a game of tennis.

He said to not worry, just get a book, read it over and meet with your kids in the fall. So I had a meeting with them and I was very honest with them. I said I don't have a whole lot of tennis knowledge. I think I can coach, I'll learn the rules, I'll learn some type of things that I can help you with, but as far as games just be patient with me. I'll try to do the best I can for you.

In prior years the team had not done well at all. In the league they were last or next-to-last out of eight teams for five straight years.

When practice started I emphasized what I felt were some key strategies. I said you can't give points away with foot faults. Get the second serve no matter how lightly you have to hit it. You work on your game, on the basics, to get better at it and we would be okay.

One thing we did have was a lot of veterans who played over two or three years coming back. We started playing and ended up fifth in the conference, so there was a little bit of improvement.

I wanted to do something, but I knew some of the other coaches probably wouldn't like it a lot. You have your players, your 1 to 6, your best players supposedly at one and your weakest player at 6. So what I did was, when we went into the tournament, I flip-flopped everything. I made my six man, my first. My fifth became second and I had my first down to six. And I did the same thing with the doubles.

We ended up in the tournament in third place. No one expected it. I know there was a coach or two that was upset with it because of my unorthodox style, but I couldn't care less. I brought happiness and confidence to these kids that they never had before at that school, at least. They were as happy as if they had won the whole thing.

We were in Bethany, West Virginia for the tournament and there was a big banquet. I was really surprised because I was named coach of year in the league!

It just kind of really surprised me and I was very happy. I think sometimes you just try to find a way to win, maybe it wasn't quite the most conventional thing to do, but it did the job.

Did I hurt the game of tennis? Did the world crash? I don't think so. I know that the seven kids that we had on that team were really happy on the way back home to Cleveland.

Game, set, match!

Viva Italia!

When I coached in Italy we had two Americans. We had Steve Poidukas, who I coached against in high school, in Chicago he was at St. Lawrence and later he was a great player at Washington State. In fact he may still hold the record for most rebounds over a career.

I also had Henry Ward, from Jackson State. One of the great leapers of all time. I've seen a lot of them, there were some great ones at Marquette, but he's up there with those. You know we had a good team.

It was difficult because I was replacing an Italian coach. Luckily I had black hair at that time, and I had a nice tan, so I looked a little Italian. We went to the playoffs, we won our first game, lost the second and it was done

It was very interesting for me because I had (beside the two Americans and the 8 Italian players) two really young Italian players. They were 18 and 19, they were pretty good but they would get nervous a lot. They never spent time preparing to play but they always asked me to come to their house for Sunday dinner.

Dinners in Italy were four hours long. Minimum. It was wonderful, I loved it! It was one of the nicest things I learned about being in the City of Cagliari on the Island of Sardinia. It was beautiful. They were great kids they just needed time and they were going to be good.

One of the great stories for me was when we went on the road for the first time, to Venice. We played the game and Henry Ward in overtime tipped in a ball after a missed free throw by us to win the game!

It was a small gym that held maybe 3500 fans. When we won they started throwing things at us. I've never seen anything like it. It's my first road game and so we head into the locker room and really happy having won.

I'm sitting there, just congratulating people. I tell them that this is one of the great wins that I've ever been a part of! So now the police come in the locker room and say "you can't leave because they have surrounded your taxi" (boat bus—because we were in Venice).

So I ask "when can we go to the taxi boat? We need to get to the hotel because the players are all tired."

So I ask the players "do you want to stay?" and they all say yes. So we sit in the locker room and wait for an hour. They finally tell us that is safe to leave, and we start walking.

I'm very happy since this is a big moment to win on the road. There's a little Italian bar and I said "come on I want everybody to have a glass of wine", so we go in there.

We're sitting in the bar and I see one of the great basketball players of all time standing there: Connie Hawkins! The Hawk is there, he's 39 or 40. I asked him what are you doing here?

He said they want him to come in for a tryout, just to play, for small money. I said man, and I must have told him 100 times, you're a great one. He said, you know Ed, I'm not a great one anymore, I just got to pay some bills.

It was very interesting because he was a chosen as one of the top 50 NBA players of all time and here he is in Italy, just trying to make a living.

Italy was truly a very interesting experience from so many standpoints.

Basketball is My Life

Every dollar I have ever made in my adult life I've made because of basketball. I feel so fortunate to be a little part of this game. This game that has been so great to a lot of people. It got me a scholarship to high school and a chance to play basketball at Marquette.

In my fifth year of school I became an assistant coach of the freshman team at Marquette. On to coaching high school basketball, for four years. Seventeen total years of coaching at the high school and collegiate level and pro ball in Italy. To go to a great company like Nike, and to eventually become Manager of College Basketball and Sports Marketing.

Back when I was right out of Marquette as a student I got my first coaching job at Saint Viator High School as a freshman/sophomore coach. I went to a basketball coaches clinic in 1968, run by Bob Murray. In those days they would rent a big ballroom with an overhead projector and the coaches would stand there with a microphone and just draw the X's and O's and speak for several hours. That's how clinics were run. They evolved from that, but I knew at that time that I wanted to do something like that.

After my first year at John Carroll I had my first coaching clinic in 1974 and I've been doing it for over 42 years. It's been something that I love to do. In some small way, to give back to the game and help these young men and women hopefully improve themselves as coaches. So they can transfer their knowledge of the game to their players and hopefully to other coaches.

When I was at Nike I was so fortunate, I was at a dinner that Nike was putting on for Michael Jordan. Sonny Vacarro, who ran basketball at Nike at that time, was there also. Michael said, kind of to everybody but pointed toward Sonny, that he'd like to run a basketball camp. Then Sonny pointed to me and that started a whole other world for me.

Fifteen years of kids camps and thirteen years of a Fantasy camp with Michael, plus working with and doing camps for other players like BJ Armstrong, Scottie Pippen and Vince Carter. It's just been a very lucky and fortunate thing for me.

Everything that I have in the world today is directly or indirectly due to basketball. And that's why I think the game is a great. It gives everybody an opportunity, if they want to go and grab it.

I Never Had a Bike

There were not very many kids that I know, even in my neighborhood, growing up in Chicago, that did not have a bike. We lived right across the street from Holstein Park, which had softball diamonds, two gyms, this is the olden days, swimming pool, anything you wanted to do, sports-wise, you had an opportunity to do it there.

When I was growing up I really didn't need a bike, I never asked for a bike and so I never had a bike, it's just one of those things.

I just didn't, and it might've been a good thing for me, everyone had to come to the park to play so I just walked across the street. I was a lucky kid to have that park across the street. Holstein Park helped me to get started in sports and life!

Holstein Park

Holstein Park became a big part of my life. I played Little League baseball, I played softball, in Chicago we have a game called 16 inch softball that we play with our bare hands. The ball starts out very very hard but then it softens up. We only played six innings.

I played a lot of softball when I was 15 with what you'd think of like a pro team in Chicago. It was a big experience for me because we traveled all over the city and I was able to go with these adults and be part of it.

The summers for me were softball and it was really important. I was playing at least six days a week and sometimes seven. There would be many games and tournaments and it was a lot of fun. All because of the park.

The summertime when I was out of school whether elementary or high school there was a school two blocks from where I lived on the other side of the park called Logan Continuation School.

The school was for students who had dropped out of high school before they were 17 years old and by law they had to go to that school twice a week, Monday to Friday, to learn some type of skill or technical job. Logan held their P.E. classes in the summertime, at the park.

Many of the black athletes would use the basketball court, so I just started hanging out there when I was 12 or 13 years old. Eventually they let me get into their pick up games.

The competition helped me a lot because I was playing against older players and better players, it definitely helped me to really learn the game.

The park really did a lot for me. The place that really brought me to loving this game of basketball, as well as softball and baseball.

Never Again!

My father was a Chicago citywide champion in speed ice-skating. When I was about 11 or 12 years old, I had not ever skated and he wanted to have me learn how to skate. I'll never forget, it was a Sunday late afternoon, he said "come on, I'm going to help you work on skating".

We went out there, and the blades on the speed skates are really long, not like hockey skates. And I'll bet you I never stood up for more than two seconds solid! I fell down so many times and after that day I never put on skates.

Fast forward to 1970 or 1971, I'm the head basketball coach at my alma mater, Weber High School. My best friend Tony Barone and his wife Kathy, myself and my wife at the time are all going to take the weekend off before practice starts, and go to this winter resort type thing.

They had everything indoors; bowling, a swimming pool, ice skating rink, all kinds of things to do for the weekend. Saturday morning they all want to go ice skating and I know I don't really want to go. I'll go there but I don't want to put the skates on.

Tony says if we go, you're going skate with all of us, so I get the skates on. They all know how to skate pretty well, and they're doing circles around the rink. I'm standing by the board just creeping along, two hands at the board, inch by inch.

There's two entrances onto the ice, I'm about halfway around to the other entrance and the lights start to flash and an announcement comes on: "Could everyone please clear the ice…Olympic champion Janet Lynn from Rockford, Illinois (where this resort was) is going to have a practice session. You're all welcome to watch."

I couldn't get off the ice, I'm still hanging on for dear life, trying to make my way around. Everyone else is off the ice and she comes on. I have got maybe thirty feet to go to get to the other entrance, now they shut the lights off, they've got the light on her and she's doing her stuff.

I can hear those three other people, Tony, my wife and Kathy, they are all laughing so hard, so everyone starts laughing. They think that I'm a joke, that I'm a clown. I finally get there and I get off the ice, I'm so embarrassed I sit down right away I took off those skates and said "NEVER AGAIN!"

A Draw!

In June of 1989, Nike was having a Las vegas 3-day photo shoot for some of it's top players. Hall of Famer Moses Malone was one the attendees and we got to be friends during the event.

The Four Tops and Frankie Valli and the Four Seasons were at the Desert Inn and Moses asked me if I wanted to go. Being a big fan of both groups I of course said yes.

Moses arranged to meet me in a limo outside our hotel. So I get in the car and it's moving slowly because there was a really big fight in town that night. It was Thomas "Hitman" Hearns vs Sugar Ray Leonard.

Moses mentioned that he had placed a bet on the fight. I immediately asked him who he took. He totally shocked me when he said he took the long odds and bet on a draw at 35-1!

I chuckled and didn't think anything more of it. We went to the show and Moses, being the big star that he was, was introduced during the show by The Four Tops. We had a great time!

Afterwards, we headed back to the hotel and went our separate ways. The next morning I pick up the paper and I can't believe the sports headline. The previous night's fight ended in a draw!

I ran into Moses a little while later and he was grinning from ear to ear. He'd bet bet $100 and walked away with $3500!

I just thought to myself, it couldn't have happened to a nicer guy. Moses was, on the court a hard working, rebounding and scoring machine. Off the court he was a real gentleman who loved to have fun.

He will be missed!

Wine Party!

We were on a Nike trip out west one time. There were a lot of great guys along. My best friend, Tony Barone and Jimmy Valvano as well as a few others. As part of the trip they had a dinner planned at a winery. The winery was about 40 minutes away and we were driven in vans that held 10-12 people.

It was a great dinner and as a gift we were all given a special bottle of wine with our name printed on it. It had been a long evening and it was time to head back to our hotel in the vans.

We're all feeling pretty good and having a lot of fun on the trip back. All of a sudden the van slows down and the driver says that the van has broken down.

Because of the late hour and where we're located the driver is having a problem reaching anyone to help us out of this jam.

Meanwhile Jimmy Valvano is holding court. As usual, he has everyone laughing at his great stories. We're stuck out in the middle of nowhere, but we're all feeling great!

Jimmy says "hey, let's open some wine"! Everyone had their personalized bottles with them, so we're opening these "keepsakes" and the party gets even better.

The driver was frantic worried about how he's going to get us out of there and we're all having a great party with wine and Jimmy's jokes keeping everybody laughing!

Finally, the replacement van came and we headed back. But, by the time we got to the hotel, the special bottles of wine had all been consumed.

What a night!

Ron Tyson

On October 17th of 2015 I celebrated a milestone birthday. On my bucket list I always wanted to have my favorite group, the Temptations, perform at a party for me. I had seen them countless times over the years and I had developed a friendship with the members of the group.

About a year and a half in advance I started planning it. I got the approval from my wife Louise, with one condition. We had to fulfill her bucket list item and renovate our home bathroom. She drives a hard bargain, but I felt that was fair. I contacted the group and arrangements were put in place to secure that date for my big event.

A lot of my old and new friends were invited, with a number of people coming in from out of town for the occasion. We arranged an evening at our house for the out of town guests the evening before the main party.

My best friend, Tony Barone and his wife Kathy, were staying at a nearby hotel. They needed a ride over to my house. I had an idea, so I called my friend Ron Tyson, a member of the Temptations for over 33 years. I asked if he was busy and if he would like to join us. He said sure, he'd be happy to come over.

I headed out to pick up everyone. I stopped to pick up Ron first and he joined me in the front seat. Then I picked up Tony and Kathy. They climbed into the back seat.

I introduced Ron to the Barones when everyone was in the car. I glanced in the rearview mirror and saw that both of the Barones were quite surprised and in awe when they realized they were riding along with "Motown royalty".

They had a great conversation in the car which continued when they got to my home. Everyone that met Ron that night was blown away by how friendly and down to earth a guy he is. I wasn't surprised at all, since I have known and been friends with the Temptations for many years. But it was fun to watch the reactions of people and see them interact.

The Golden Jet

When I was a kid growing up in Chicago every other Sunday they would have a bus, sponsored by our neighborhood bar, The Return Tap, that would take a group to a Chicago Blackhawks game at the old Chicago Stadium. I always remember, as I am sure every kid did, that the old Stadium held 16,666 people.

They would seat us all together. They weren't the best seats in the house, but they were pretty good ones. We were all sports fans so it didn't matter where we were, we were just happy to be there experiencing this event.

The Blackhawks at the time had the great Bobby Hull playing for them. Arguably the best player to ever play for the Hawks and one of the greatest of all time anywhere.

It was spellbinding to watch, when Hull would get the puck behind his net and start his rush down the ice, the whole place started to become electrified. Everyone would be out of their seats in anticipation of what Hull was about to do. Whether it was just a pass or taking a shot it was fascinating to watch one of the greats do his thing.

Years later, in the same arena, I had the privilege and pleasure to watch a similar occurrence. The great Michael Jordan would get the ball under his net and make his way down court. A similar reaction would come from the crowd, especially in crunch time, as they rise to their feet expecting something great to happen.

To me, there are only a select few in my lifetime, that can make something like that happen and change the outcome of a game single handedly.

Hull & Jordan, two Chicago icons!

Lesson Learned

When I was in my mid teens, around fifteen or sixteen, I used to make a few bucks in the summer playing softball. I also made some money pitching pennies, nickels and even some quarters, but that's another story.

In the months before I was going off to college I got a summer job in a paint factory. I still played a lot of softball in the evenings and on weekends.

One of the teams I played for was sponsored by the local bar, the Return Tap. It was owned by a guy named Joe Puhopec.

One hot day in August, I was walking by the bar and Joe gave me a coke. One of the regulars there, a fellow by the name of Stash, asked me if I wanted to go to Arlington Park. I had never been so I said of course. We hopped in a taxi and a short while later we were at the track.

We headed over to the paddock and he spent the next fifteen minutes intently staring at each of the horses. He didn't say a word to me the whole time. He just kept looking at each of the horses.

Finally he motions me to follow him and we head to the ticket window. He places a $50 bet on a horse to win. The odds were 8-1, if I remember correctly.

We headed to the stands and I got to watch my first live horse race. Wow, it was exciting from start to finish, unbelievably, his horse won.

We headed over to the counter and he picked up his winnings. Next he turned to me and said, okay let's go. I was dumbfounded. I couldn't believe we were leaving already and asked him why we weren't making another bet on the next race.

He just said to me: "that's why I win!"

It's a good lesson when it comes to gambling. I just wish that I had paid more attention to it in the years since!

Cubs New Reliever

Sometime in the late sixties or early seventies, Tony Barone and his wife and my wife and I went to my wife's parents' cottage in Indiana. It was a beautiful cottage on Clear Lake. The parents were quite strict and they didn't think that a cottage should have a TV, so they didn't have one.

Tony and I were longtime Cubs fans (and still are..Go Cubbies). They were scheduled to play the next afternoon and of course we wanted to see the game. The wives had other plans for us, wanting to go for a ride on a pontoon boat, but we managed to wiggle our way out of that.

The next door neighbor was a friendly guy by the name of Tom Shank who said that we could come over to his cottage anytime that we wanted to watch TV.

So the next day Tony and I are excited to go over and we get comfortable and turn the TV on. However, there is no sound. Neither Tony nor I are technical guys so we can't figure out how to get the sound on the TV set.

As we are watching, at one point we see that the Cubs are sending out a reliever to the mound. I notice that as he is walking out they have a name running under him on the TV screen. I knew my players back then and I turned to Tony and said I don't know this guy. I ask him who is "Audio Difficulties"?

Tony starts laughing so hard that he almost falls off his chair and he says to me: "it's audio difficulties, NO SOUND DUMMY!"

Well, at least that finally explained why we had no sound!

Wapatoolie

I have great friends and great memories from Marquette University over the years. One of my great recollections involves what we used to call the Wapatoolie Party.

One year during my Marquette days I lived in a house with seven other guys. There were four bedrooms, two of us in each one. They were all great guys and we got along really well.

The house had a very large basement. Which, let's just say, was conducive for parties. We had a party, which in Milwaukee, was called a Wapatoolie party. It was a very simple concept. If you were invited all you had to bring was a quart of liquor. It didn't matter what kind you brought, just as long as you brought alcohol, you were admitted to the party.

Once you handed over your bottle we would pour it into the very large container and we would add another two quarts of juice. Orange juice, pineapple juice or whatever we had would all go into, what was usually, a giant plastic garbage can.

Lots of ice, too. Usually it was filled half way up with ice before we even got started. We also had an old boat paddle and that's what we would use to stir all of the ingredients together.

One of the housemates, Billy Daniher, managed to get a jukebox which was driven in from Chicago. We had Motown, Rock & Roll, soul music and all of our other favorites ready to party the night away.

The only problem that we ran into was that the beverages flowed a little too easily. With all the juice it made for a very sweet conception. You'd dip your own glass in and help yourself. Well, after a couple of these you'd suddenly get a reaction.

Needless to say there were a lot of very intoxicated people. All of a sudden our house had a lot more people spending the night.

But the event was always a lot of fun. I'm sure not much different from one college to another right across the country. Ours just happened to be called Wapatoolie!

Heckling the Fan!

Hubie Brown, a Hall of Famer in every way you could imagine, has a lot of stories. I asked him why he has never written a book and he said he's had a lot of basketball books sent to him over the years. In fact there are enough to fill a nice long shelf in his home. But, he says he hasn't read many of them.

He told me he will let his wife write his book after he is gone. She knows all the stories and he probably wouldn't even read his own book if he wrote it.

There's one story that would probably be in her book that he has told a few times. He was coaching Memphis and they were playing the Knicks at Madison Square Garden. As usual it was a noisy crowd and they were beating the Knicks by a lot.

Some loud mouth starts to harass Shane Battier, his starting forward at the time. He walked up to the stands where this guy was sitting and asked who was yelling this stuff out.

Unbelievably, at least for the Garden, it got very quiet all of a sudden. Hubie started to scold this fan. He told him if he had a son he would be lucky if he had even half the class that Shane Battier had.

That shut the fan up.

Hubie Brown, still working hard in his eighties!

Shorten Up

When I graduated from eighth grade, I was fortunate enough to get a basketball scholarship to Weber High School. Weber was a member of the Catholic League, which, at that time, was not a member of the state association.

There were 13 schools playing by different rules. By different rules I mean you could practice whenever you wanted to. You could give out scholarships to attract the best players, etc.

But they also had something very unique in basketball. In all the history before the mid 70's they called their varsity team the heavyweights. Then they had the bantams which would be the freshman and sophomore teams. Then they would have another area called the lightweights which were players 5' and under and the freshman sophomore team for the lightweights would be called the flyweights. So it was really kind of unusual but it gave a chance for the smaller players, height wise anyway, to play the game.

If you chose to, you could go to be measured. Well, when I got to my senior year, they moved the measurement for the junior varsity, the smaller players, to be 5'9" and under. So I was about 5'10 ½" or 5'11" at that time and I made a decision. I went to the varsity coach, because if you made height, you could play on both teams. You could play on the junior varsity which was really a varsity team, and also play on the varsity team.

So every year there would be 3-5 of our guys that would try to lose height. The measuring in would always be at Fenwick high school in Oak Park, Illinois.

You would start off Wednesday in the morning when you came to school by standing in the back of the classroom instead of sitting at your desk. The teachers and the priests all knew that you were going to try to lose height.

Some guys would take 2 bowling balls, one in each hand, and stand there throughout the class. One of the guys would have a classmate on his shoulders and stand during class.

This would go on through the regular class day. Now this was Wednesday night and you would do the same type of things when you went home. You did not sit down, you would stand up as long as you could and some guys were able to make it through the night, some guys weren't and they would have to start again. On Thursday we would go through the same situation, but on Thursday night you would meet up with the other players and we would walk all the way to downtown Chicago – you would stay on your feet – always on your feet. Then Friday comes and you're doing the same thing in the classroom.

A lot of the guys, if they had the good strength, would have the guys on their shoulders. Then the school bus would take us to the measuring area at Fenwick High School and guys standing on the bus had other students on their shoulders and their heads were hitting the top of the bus.

We went there and 2 or 3, of the 4 or 5 made it. However, I did not. The amazing thing is, when we got back to school after the measuring in, there was a sock hop going on at that time. You would think that we would be going home to bed, but no, we went to that sock hop and had a great time.

Oh to be young again, that's all I can say!

Coach K

Coach Mike Krzyzewski and I went to the same high school in Chicago. I was two years ahead of him. He was an outstanding high school player, especially in his senior year. He made the All City Team which is a great honor in Chicago, obviously, and then he went on to the army to play for Coach Bob Knight.

Bob converted Mike to point guard which made him one of the tallest point guards in collegiate basketball. They had great success there. By the way, Mike averaged 25 points per game in high school, and never scored 25 points for coach Knight but he had a great, great career there as both of them moved on and it was the influence of Coach Knight to help Mike be where he is today as the top of the college basketball world.

On the social side of it, Mike is a big fan of Smokey Robinson. We were in Las Vegas for either a clinic or a fantasy camp. Smokey was playing at Caesars Palace and I knew some people there and I got some great seats.

I could see that Mike was really enjoying the show and then after the show I arranged for us go to the green room to see Smokey. It was very interesting when we got there.

We waited a couple of minutes and Smokey came out in his robe. When Mike and he met, they shook hands and Smokey said "it's a real pleasure to meet you" and Mike said, "Smokey, you helped me get through West Point, I really appreciated that, I love your music". Then they had a nice little conversation.

It just shows what happens when people come together what great things can happen and I know it was a meeting of two different great minds and two very special people.

Stations

We always had a session at the Michael Jordan Senior Flight School called stations – each one of the coaching staff would be at a basket and the teams would rotate in timed intervals to each coach. The main purpose of each station was to have a different drill focusing on a specific aspect of the game.

Each of the coaches was also assigned a team that played under that coach for the duration of the camp. It was interesting to see the philosophy of each of the coaches.

Quite often a coach would treat his own team much differently than the others when they reached his particular station. Sometimes the coach would run a quick practice session with his team. Other times he might just have his players take a mini rest period. In either case they were not doing the assigned drill that was supposed to be worked on.

However, when the other teams would get to some coach's station, they would work them very hard at that particular drill and believe me, some of these drills were not easy!

You've got to understand these campers who were there, are anywhere from 35 to 70 years old. It's a long day and some coaches wanted to get the opposing teams even more tired before his team would play them later in the day.

They were breaking the rules, but in a good natured way. These coaches are all very competitive and they were always looking for an advantage over the other coaches.

People like to try to win in different ways.

Coaches at Camp (Part 1)

As I mentioned in a previous story, the Michael Jordan Senior Flight School had an outstanding great coaching staff all the years we had the camp. It was just amazing!

When I got the idea to start the camp the only concern that I had was how competitive would these great coaches be at a summer basketball camp. You really didn't know, I ran camps, I've seen camps, some coaches take a different view of things. This is not what they do for their careers, so you didn't know what was going to happen.

In the first year of camp, part of the coaching staff was Coach Mike Krzyzewski and Coach Dean Smith. It was the first day of games and I was over at another court. It just so happened that the opening game was Mike's team versus Dean's team and obviously they had a strong rivalry in the ACC and you just didn't know what was going to happen.

I was on another court and all of a sudden there is a commotion going on on the other side of the gym on another court and I looked over and I see players, coaches and people all up. I get over there and the officials made a call and I don't know if it was Dean or Mike that didn't like the call but whatever happened all of a sudden I see Mike and Dean face to face going at each other a little bit.

I said to myself, I don't have to worry about the competitiveness of camp anymore because these guys came to win – they want to win the game. That's what their life has been all about and that's what they're going to show these campers.

Coaches at Camp (Part 2)

Another humorous storey about Michael's Camp was based around our policy of having co-coaches. We would put coaches together and Bob Huggins and Hubie Brown were always matched up together as co-coaches.

But you know, obviously Hubie with a lot more experience, especially in the NBA, so he took a stronger leadership role in the coaching part of it. In this particular year, Bob and Hubie did not have the best team.

They were playing a game where they were down towards the end of the third quarter by 20 points and we had a rule that if you were ever down 15 points or more you could press.

Well Hubie was getting very upset at his players. He wanted to take a little time and he moved off towards the end of the bench and Bob kind of took over and he threw in a little press here and there and all of a sudden, what do you know, with the last possession of the third quarter, his team cuts it down to 15.

Then we started the 4th quarter and I'm watching this because it is very interesting. Bob has his team out there and they press again and they steal the ball and got a 3 point play out of it. All of a sudden their team is only down 12 and now they are starting to play well offensively on the half court and before you know it, it's down to 5 or 6.

All of a sudden there is a time out called. Hubie comes from the end of the bench and comes right out and takes over the reins again. I didn't stay for the rest of the game and I don't know if they won or lost but it just shows the competitiveness. He wasn't going to stand on the sideline and not do something. He took a little time away from the players and then got back into it and he gave Bob an opportunity to coach the team.

There was always something interesting to remember the camps by.

Denny McLain

When I was in high school, my freshman year, we played our first season of baseball at Weber High School. We actually got our uniforms from the Chicago Cubs, which were their former spring training uniforms.

Our head coach was a fellow by the name of Jim Righeimer, who was also the line coach for the football team. He was a very tough, good man and a good coach.

Baseball in Chicago in the spring time is something where you have to deal with the weather all the time and we played a lot in very, very cold weather… 30 or 35 degrees, sometimes even snow flurries.

Our second or third game of the season was against Mt. Carmel High School. They had a pitcher by the name of Denny McLain. About eight years later, in 1968, McLain became the last pitcher in Major League Baseball to win 30 or more games during a season (31–6)— a feat accomplished by only eleven players in the 20th century.

He threw the ball using an over the top motion fastball. It was unbelievable. He also had a strange habit that we noticed during the game. Between innings, when his team went to the bench, he would finish off a whole 16oz Pepsi.

It was incredible to watch this guy. In that game, I started at first base and I batted third. I batted against him 3 times, I struck out all 3 times, never touching the ball.

As a team we only had 2 hits: a bunt for a hit, and a swinging bunt. We had a chance to see how great this guy was in his high school years and obviously when he went on to the major leagues. He had one of the last great season pitching records.

I doubt that will ever happen again – no one will ever win 30 games again because the game has changed and pitchers don't have the same opportunities.

To me, I look back on it as a great day! I had a chance to play against one of the outstanding pitchers of all time – Denny McLain.

Important People!

Geno Auriemma - He's a Hall of Famer who will be remembered as the greatest women's basketball coach of all time, but believe me he could be a division one men's coach and even an NBA coach if he wanted to.

Charles Barkley - Funny, smart, speaks his mind, but a great player. For his size what he did was astronomical in my opinion. A Hall of Famer!

Jim Boeheim - Never has received his due, as far as I am concerned from the populous. He has done so much; stayed at one school as a player and Hall of Fame Coach for over 50 years...and he did it the right way, no matter what anyone thinks.

Doug Bruno - A good friend of mine, head coach at DePaul. He was also an assistant at Loyola. He made DePaul women's basketball what it is today.

Jim Calhoun - Took Connecticut from the bottom of the Big East to the top of the Big East. A great motivator, excellent coach and won three national championships.

Lou Carnesecca - One of the nicest people to ever coach the game. What I learned from him was Long Island Apples. You wonder what that is? You've got to ask me when you see me.

John Chaney - Temple coach – continued the great tradition at Temple in his way, a tough man. 6:00 a.m. practices I loved to go to them.

Sherri Coale - Right from high school to the University of Oklahoma as head coach and built that program into a national power. One of the top women's coaches and an outstanding teacher of the game.

Bobby Cremins - Great guy, wonderful human being. Took Georgia Tech from the bottom of the ACC to the top. I'd like to see him be in the Hall of Fame, I don't know if he can make it or not but he's a guys' guy, an Irish New Yorker.

Chuck Daly - Made his mark with the Bad Boys. Could coach and could make his team a family. Olympic Gold with the Dream Team. Hall of Famer!

Cliff Ellis - This year will be close to 800 wins, unfortunately not known to some people west of the Mississippi, but has done a great job with several programs. Stands the test of time!

Bob Huggins - a great friend, a loyal friend, outstanding coach, old school, does it his way, a proven winner. Hall of Famer to be.

Sam Jones - Greatest bank shooter of all time, Hall of Famer. I was just happy to have him as a friend.

Gene Keady - A man's man who coached the way you would want your son or daughter to be coached by someone. A winner; a guy who took Purdue to the top.

Phil Knight - Founder and former President, CEO of Nike; innovator, played on the edge, no fear, wanted to be a winner, became a winner, helped make Oregon a winner.

Mike Krzyzewski - greatest men's basketball coach of all time – when this book is being written he is chasing his third Olympic gold. A coach's coach. Does it the right way. He was my high school classmate and a friend.

Eric Lautenbach - I hired him at Nike. Has become one of Nike's most valuable employee; Nike's connection to College basketball and the Olympic games basketball team. Valuable, honest and a good person. Our friendship is special!

Abe Lemons - The funniest, most humorous coach that's ever coached a game. He deserved more than he got – I love him.

Moses Malone - Rebounder, good guy, tough guy but he always was a nice person anytime you met him.

Rick Majerus - A great friend, great coach loved to share ideas about the game, loved to teach the game, made every player he's ever coached better. You can't say that about too many people. Left us too soon.

Gerry "Magoo" McGinty - Has been working with me for over 35 years at my coaches clinics; a difference maker with his hard work, his socialization and his basketball knowledge. Former coach, former athletic director. I thank him forever.

Phil Martelli - Coach at St. Josephs. Underrated! Has given most of his coaching life to one school and he's the best guy for that school. Really a good person.

Bob McKillop - Davidson, Long Island New York high school coach. He has coached Davidson since 1989. Does a great job – goes overseas and does clinics and he's taken a small program and built it into a nationally recognized successful program.

Frank McGuire - Some may not have heard of him but he brought north eastern basketball style, especially New York

City to the south, a great coach, collegiately and professionally.

Dave Odom - Has been successful wherever he has been, as an assistant or as a head coach! At Wake Forest, really taught Tim Duncan how to play the game. A great teacher.

Lute Olson - He did it the right way; made Arizona what it is today; from the bottom of the PAC 10 and PAC 12 to the top. Tough to beat him anytime, anywhere.

Bill Raftery - One of the real sweet human beings, a good coach underrated coach but one of the great announcers of all time. I mean he has made it exciting, truthful with a sense of humor, one of the great banquet speakers of all time and I'm happy that I can call him a friend.

Jack Ramsay - Hall of Famer, creator, outstanding coach at St. Joe's and especially when he won the 1977 NBA Championship with the Portland Trail Blazers.

George Raveling - A member of the Basketball Hall of Fame, outstanding coach, co-director The Michael Jordan Senior Flight School. Was a big part in making it what it was. Has only done positive things to make the game better.

Bill Self - Obviously an outstanding coach and national champion; will be in the hall of fame. He was with Nike when he was at Kansas for a while then Kansas switched but he has always been a good friend and I just wanted to see him be successful. Hall of Famer to be!

Dean Smith - An innovator, changed so much in the game, run and jump, huddles at the foul line, one of the great coaches of all time in any sport.

Tubby Smith - Did something special at Kentucky, a wonderful human being, but more importantly, showed that things can change at certain universities. Builder of programs.

Eddie Sutton - Arkansas, Kentucky, Oklahoma State, in the beginning Creighton, always made his program a winner, always. Should be in the Hall of Fame.

Jerry Tarkanian - As I said about Phil Knight, this guy played on the edge of things, but you know what, he was a winner and that's what you do in Las Vegas.

John Thompson - Hall of Famer, created Georgetown into a national program, did something rare, coming from high school right to college and making Georgetown a great program. NCAA Champions.

Gary Williams - The most intense coach I have ever been around but more importantly, one of the nicest people I have ever been around. Returned to his alma mater, Maryland, to win a national championship.

Sonny Vaccaro - Changed the game of shoes and equipment in basketball. Made coaches a lot of money, helped many kids, gave me a big chance.

Tara Vanderveer - one of the great women's basketball coaches in history. A pioneer for the modern women's success in the Olympics. She took a select team for an entire year and went undefeated and brought home the Olympic gold. Stanford's best ever and a member of the basketball Hall of Fame.

Roy Williams - worked for one of the greatest , Dean Smith, rebuilt a dynasty at Kansas, came back home to North Carolina and won two National Championships. A true gentleman and a Hall of Famer.

John Wooden - Obviously, the winningest NCAA championship coach in history! His record will never be surpassed. Spoke at my second clinic that I ever had in my life; a great gentleman that is revered by many, many people.

Jay Wright - Besides being one of the best dressed coaches, he has done a magnificent job in making Villanova once again a national power and the 2016 NCAA Champs.

Thank you

I want to say a special thanks to all those people who have helped me in my life, in my basketball life, in my life at Nike.

Obviously the coaches, who I've met, worked with, the NBA players, all those who have helped me with my coaching clinics, the camps that I have run, especially the Fantasy Camps, the people at Nike who were so good to me since 1982 when I started the clinics and 15 great years of working in Beaverton.

I also want to thank my lifelong friends from Marquette University who have always supported me and whose friendships are so dear to me.

A big thank you to my wife, Louise, for her patience and support of me over the years!

Also, I'm not going to forget the players, coaches and friends who are in heaven.

Thank you all!